A Celebration of Psalms for Kids

Mary J. Davis

LEGACY PRESS®

To some of the most important "girls" in my life:
My sisters – Kathy, Margie, Carol, Barb and Norma
My daughters – Lori and Wendi
Aunt Lynn and Holly
Margie, Gwen and Amanda

MY PRAISE JOURNAL
©2007 by Legacy Press, seventh printing
ISBN 10: 1-885358-71-7
ISBN 13: 978-1-885358-71-4
Legacy reorder #LP46921
JUVENILE NONFICTION/Religion/Devotion & Prayer

Illustrator: Aline Heiser

Legacy Press
P.O. Box 261129
San Diego, CA 92196

Printed in the United States of America

Table of contents

Introduction 5
Chapter 1 7
Great and Worthy 8
I Will Tell Others 10
Fearfully and Wonderfully Made 12
You Know Me 14
You Daily Bear Our Burdens 16
I Will Sing with My Soul 18
I Will Sing Praises All My Life 20
I Will Sing About My Awesome God! 22
Shout His Praise! 24
I Cannot Be Silent 26
Songs of Joy 28
The Righteous Rejoice 30
Song of Thanksgiving .32
Praise You in Your House 34
Praise Out Loud 36
Chapter 2 39
Serve the Lord 40
A Servant Redeemed .42
Guide My Hand, Lord .44
A Blameless Servant 46
I Love Your Laws, God 48
Clean Hands 50
The Godly Pray 52
He Hears My Prayers .54
Your Flawless Word 56
A Light for My Path 58
Worship with Gladness 60
Give Glory 62
Worship in God's House 64
I Will Tell Others 66
Tell of Your Righteousness 68
Tell of Your Deeds 70

Chapter 3 .... **73**
  I Trust You 74
  Trusting When I'm Afraid 76
  Those Who Trust in Other Things 78
  I Keep Trusting 80
  My Strength 82
  Praise to the Lord, My Strength 84
  You Hold My Hand 86
  My Hiding Place 88
  You Are Faithful 90
  I Love You, Lord 92
  You Love Me with a Forever Love 94
  Unfailing Love 96
  Even Me 98
  My Rock and My Salvation 100
  Rejoice in Salvation 102
  My Savior 104
  Saved by Your Son 106
  My Father 108
  A Father to the Fatherless 110
  My Protector 112
  My Shepherd 114
Chapter 4 .... **117**
  Praise Your Holy Name 118
  My God Is Holy 120
  How Majestic Is Your Name! 122
  The Majesty of My God 124
  My God Reigns 126
  My God Reigns Forever 128
  My God Is Everlasting 130
  My God's Love Is Everlasting 132
  Mighty God 134
  My Creator 136
  My God Is Faithful 138
Psalms to Memorize **141**
In Conclusion **143**

Introduction

Psalms is a wonderful book. It is filled with advice, cries for help, thanksgiving for help given, laughter, tears and lots of praise.

Psalms is the longest book in the Bible. It was written by several different people. In *My Praise Journal*, a writer of a psalm is referred to as a "psalmist." In your Bible, you will see the name of the person who wrote that psalm at the beginning of each chapter. David wrote many of the Psalms. You will notice that some of the chapters have headings to tell you why they were written.

God loves to hear the praises of His children. *My Praise Journal* will help you praise God. You will learn to praise Him in all of life's situations. Each part of this journal is designed to help you learn God's Word and find ways to praise Him in all that you do.

To make the best use of this journal, follow these steps:

Read the Word

Read the passage from Psalms. You might want to read the verses more than once. Many of the psalms are beautiful to read and think about.

Think About the Word

This section gives you a short explanation of the verses you just read. It will help you know why the verses are important to your own life.

Live the Word

Writing helps people remember what they learn. Write the answers to the questions in this section so you will have a better understanding of the lesson.

My Praises

You are given several lines to write your praises in this section. Don't list the same praises every time — be creative!

Pray About the Word

A prayer is suggested for you in this section to read and pray. You may also use this as a prayer starter, and just keep enjoying talking to God.

Use the Word

You may be asked to write a poem to God in this section. Or you may be encouraged to memorize a verse. This section will help you use the Word of God in your everyday life.

There are two important sections at the end of the book. Check out "Psalms to Memorize" on page 141. This is a list of psalms that you can learn to remember so you know them when you need them. Also, don't forget about "In Conclusion" on page 143. This is where you write your final thoughts about your work in this book.

Now that you know how to read through *My Praise Journal*, it is time to get started. Take the advice of Psalm 119:11 ("I have hidden your word in my heart that I might not sin against you.") and fill your heart and mind with God's precious Word.

Chapter 1

Great and Worthy

Read the Word

Great is the Lord and most worthy of praise; his greatness no one can fathom.

— Psalm 145:3

Think About the Word

Fathom means beyond understanding. The verse says that God's greatness is more than we could begin to understand. He is worthy of your praise.

Live the Word

Who do you know that you would call a great person?

_____

_____

_____

_____

What makes this person great?

_____

_____

_____

_____

What do you think makes God's greatness beyond understanding?

_____

_____

_____

My Praises

_____

_____

_____

Pray About the Word

God, You are worthy of our praise. It says so in Your Word, and I feel it in my heart. My mind cannot begin to realize just how wonderful, loving and merciful that You are. I love You very much! Amen.

Use the Word

Make a list of words you can use to describe the greatness of God.

Remember to praise God every chance you get this week!

_____

_____

_____

_____

I Will Tell Others

Read the Word

I will praise you, O Lord, with all my heart; I will tell of all your wonders. I will be glad and rejoice in you; I will sing praise to your name, O Most High.

— Psalm 9:1-2

Think About the Word

Sometimes it seems like God's greatness and His love are the world's best-kept secrets. After all, if everyone knew God personally and understood how great He is, they would be too busy praising Him to be involved in sins and selfishness. Everyone would be telling everyone else about God's greatness.

Live the Word

List some ways the world might change if everyone were busy praising God and telling others of His greatness.

_____

_____

_____

My Praises

_____

_____

_____

Pray About the Word

I promise with all my heart, Lord, that I will tell others of Your greatness. I will share Your love with all those around me, and those I meet. Amen.

Use the Word

Make a list of God's blessings in your life. Then write how you can praise Him. Tell at least one person this week about God's love and His greatness.

_____

_____

_____

Fearfully and Wonderfully Made

Read the Word

For you created my inmost being; you knit me together in my mother's womb. I praise you because I am fearfully and wonderfully made; your works are wonderful, I know that full well. My frame was not hidden from you when I was made in the secret place. When I was woven together in the depths of the earth, your eyes saw my unformed body. All the days ordained for me were written in your book before one of them came to be.

— Psalm 139:13-16

Think About the Word

Do you ever feel worthless or hopeless? Do you wish you looked differently? All people have those feelings at times. But God wants us to know WITHOUT A DOUBT that you are fearfully and wonderfully made. He took great care in creating you.

Live the Word

What do you think is the best thing about you?

_____

_____

_____

_____

_____

How can God use that best thing for His glory?

_____

_____

_____

_____

My Praises

_____

_____

_____

Pray About the Word

God, I love to read the words "I praise you because I am fearfully and wonderfully made; your works are wonderful." That verse makes me feel so special. How much better could I be, if You made me in Your own wonderful way? Thank You for giving me these verses to help me feel good about myself. I praise You, God! Amen.

Use the Word

On a blank piece of paper, make a list of things about yourself that you grumble about. Now, write OVER that list with a dark marker: I AM FEARFULLY AND WONDERFULLY MADE! Put this paper on a mirror or your dresser and look at it often. Remember that God made you just the way He wanted, and He will use you for His glory.

You Know Me

Read the Word

O Lord, you have searched me and you know me. You know when I sit and when I rise; you perceive my thoughts from afar. You discern my going out and my lying down; you are familiar with all my ways. Before a word is on my tongue you know it completely, O Lord.

— Psalm 139:1-4

Think About the Word

A girl and her best friend knew each other so well that they would actually finish each others' sentences. Many times twins can sense when the other is in trouble or sick. But God knows everything about you. He even knows your thoughts that are never spoken out loud. Verse 1 above says, "You have searched me and you know me." God takes the time to search your soul and know you in the most personal way. Nobody on earth could ever know you that well.

Live the Word

List things God understands about you that others may not.

_____

_____

_____

_____

_____

My Praises

_____

_____

_____

Pray About the Word

At times, Lord, I feel that nobody understands me or knows what I really am feeling. I will remember from now on that there is someone who really knows me and really understands. Thank You. I praise You! Amen.

Use the Word

On a blank piece of paper, write a story about yourself. Write your feelings, likes, dislikes and dreams for the future. Do you have a secret dream that nobody knows about? Write your story as though it will be read by someone who has never met you.

_____

_____

_____

_____

_____

⭐

You Daily Bear Our Burdens

Read the Word

Praise be to the Lord, to God our Savior, who daily bears our burdens.
— Psalm 68:19

Think About the Word

How many times have you felt that you cannot carry a burden any longer? Parents expect a lot from you, teachers expect a lot, friends expect a lot. You even expect a lot from yourself! The verse above says that God "daily" bears your burdens. The verse doesn't mean that God will make your parents stop expecting you to do certain things, or that your teacher will not care what kind of grades you get. It means that God will help you do what is expected of you. God doesn't want you to carry a heavy load all by yourself.

Live the Word

Write at least two burdens that you can allow God to bear for you.

_____

_____

_____

_____

How can you obey and love those around you while allowing God to help you with your burdens?

_____

_____

_____

_____

My Praises

_____

_____

_____

_____

_____

_____

Pray About the Word

God, thank You so much for this verse. I needed to hear it. I needed to know that You are here with me each and every day, helping me to carry the burdens that seem so unfair and so heavy at times. I love You! Amen.

Use the Word

Write out one burden that seems too heavy for you to carry alone. Now write the verse below the burden. How could God help you handle the burden more easily?

_____

_____

_____

_____

_____

_____

_____

_____

I Will Sing with My Soul

Read the Word

My heart is steadfast, O God; I will sing and make music with all my soul. Awake, harp and lyre! I will awaken the dawn. I will praise you, O Lord, among the nations; I will sing of you among the peoples. For great is your love, higher than the heavens; your faithfulness reaches to the skies. Be exalted, O God, above the heavens, and let your glory be over all the earth.

— Psalm 108:1-5

Think About the Word

What a happy Scripture! How could anyone feel down or worried while repeating these verses to God? Read it over and over, until you feel that your soul is filled with praises to God.

Live the Word

What is higher than the heavens?

_____

_____

_____

_____

_____

What reaches to the skies?

_____

_____

_____

_____

My Praises

_____

_____

_____

Pray About the Word

I feel like singing when I read these verses, God. I love to think
of how great You are and just let my whole body praise You,
deep down into my soul. Your love is great! Your faithfulness to
Your children is beyond measure. You are a great and
wonderful God! Amen.

Use the Word

Write out four or five "I will's" of your own. For example
"I will remind my parents of Your great love."

_____

_____

_____

_____

_____

I Will Sing Praises All My Life

Read the Word

I will sing to the Lord all my life; I will sing praise to my God as long as I live. May my meditation be pleasing to him, as I rejoice in the Lord.
— Psalm 104:33-34

Think About the Word

Your whole life is a long time. Can you remember doing something five years ago, or even last year, that you still do? Ask a parent or other adult what they praise God about.

Live the Word

What things do you praise God for now?

_____

_____

_____

_____

_____

What do you think you will praise God for when you are an adult?

_____

_____

_____

_____

My Praises

_____

_____

Pray About the Word

Father, I praise You now and I will continue to praise You all my life. I look forward to seeing how You bless me and guide me throughout the years of my life! Amen.

Use the Word

Write a song to God. An easy way to do this is to write new words to a familiar tune, or you may choose to make up the tune also.

_____

_____

_____

I Will Sing About My Awesome God!

Read the Word

(1) Shout with joy to God, all the earth! (2) Sing the glory of his name; make his praise glorious! (3) Say to God, "How awesome are your deeds! So great is your power that your enemies cringe before you. (4) All the earth bows down to you; they sing praise to you, they sing praise to your name.

— Psalm 66:1-4

Think About the Word

We truly have an awesome God! The whole earth is told to shout with joy, sing God's glory and even to bow down to God! The whole entire earth! That is awesome, don't you think?

Live the Word

Read all four verses above at least once. Write the first word of the first three verses here:

1. _____

2. _____

3. _____

Write all of verse 3 here.

_____

_____

_____

In verse 4, who bows to God?

_____

_____

_____

⭐

My Praises

_____

_____

_____

Pray About the Word

God, what can I say that is not already written in Your Word? You are awesome! You are powerful and all-knowing. You are loving and merciful. But best of all, God, You are mine! I love You! Amen.

Use the Word

Write at least ten words below to describe God.

_____

_____

_____

_____

_____

_____

_____

_____

_____

_____

☆

Shout His Praise!

Read the Word

Shout for joy to the Lord, all the earth, burst into jubilant song with music; make music to the Lord with the harp, with the harp and the sound of singing, with trumpets and the blast of the ram's horn – shout for joy before the Lord, the King.

— Psalm 98:4-6

Think About the Word

Jill goes to a church that does not believe in clapping or applauding during or after a song. Kelli's church does not have a piano or other instruments. Sarah's church has a praise band. At Misty's church, people often stand in the middle of a song or prayer and lift their hands to God. Which of these ways of praising are correct? Which are wrong? The answer to both questions is "none." There is no right or wrong way to praise God, as long as your heart is right with Him.

Live the Word

List the different ways of praising that are included in the verses above.

_____

_____

_____

_____

Write about how your church praises God.

_____

_____

_____

_____

My Praises

_____

_____

_____

_____

_____

Pray About the Word

I will sing and shout praises to You, God. I sometimes just want to burst out in a loud song. There are times when I want to shout, "God loves me and I am glad!" Thank You for showing me in Your Word that there are many ways to praise You. Amen.

Use the Word

Make up a cheerleading chant to praise God. Write it down and put it where you can see it each day. Get some friends together and teach them your cheer.

☆

I Cannot Be Silent

Read the Word

You…clothed me with joy, that my heart may sing to you and not be silent. O Lord my God, I will give you thanks forever.

— Psalm 30:11-12

Think About the Word

Have you ever been so excited about something that you couldn't keep quiet about it? Perhaps someone special was coming to visit, or you received a very special gift. The excitement over something very special makes you want to tell everyone around you, doesn't it?

Live the Word

Write about one of those times when you were so excited about something you couldn't keep quiet about it.

_____

_____

_____

_____

_____

_____

God gives such joy that it is hard to keep silent. Your heart wants to sing with all that joy bubbling right out!

My Praises

_____

_____

_____

Pray About the Word

God, it is so wonderful to have such a joy-filled heart that I have to sing praises to You. I will thank You forever and ever. Amen.

Use the Word

Cut a heart from plain paper. (If you fold the paper in half, it is easy to cut half a heart, then unfold to a whole heart.) Write all of the verse at left on the heart. Put the heart on your bedroom door or near your bed.

You...clothed me with joy,
that my heart may sing to you
and not be silent.
O Lord my God,
I will give you thanks
forever.
Psalm 30:11-12

Songs of Joy

Read the Word

When the Lord brought back the captives to Zion, we were like men who dreamed. Our mouths were filled with laughter, our tongues with songs of joy. Then it was said among the nations, "The Lord has done great things for them." The Lord has done great things for us, and we are filled with joy. Restore our fortunes, O Lord, like streams in the Negev. Those who sow in tears will reap with songs of joy. He who goes out weeping, carrying seed to sow, will return with songs of joy, carrying sheaves with him.

— Psalm 126

Think About the Word

You may have an enemy (a problem in your life) to be conquered. You often have other needs (healing of an illness or money to provide a needed item). Even with the everyday things that you need, you can be sure that God will meet those needs. We all have many reasons to sing songs of joy. What a wonderful God we have!

Live the Word

The psalmist has many reasons to sing songs of joy. God did many great things in the verses above. Underline the phrase "songs of joy" three times in the verses. Write at least two things that God did for the people.

_____

_____

_____

_____

My Praises

_____

_____

_____

Pray About the Word

God, You take such good care of me. Everyday I can see ways that You meet my needs. I will sing songs of joy to You all my life. Amen.

Use the Word

Begin to sing praises to God everyday. You will find that life is much happier when you do. Your problems will seem smaller. God will bless you.

The Righteous Rejoice

Read the Word

May God arise, may his enemies be scattered; may his foes flee before him. As smoke is blown away by the wind, may you blow them away; as wax melts before the fire, may the wicked perish before God. But may the righteous be glad and rejoice before God; may they be happy and joyful.

— Psalm 68:1-3

Think About the Word

Enemies of God are those who do not love Him or obey His Word. The righteous are those who follow in God's ways.

Live the Word

Write three things that will happen to God's enemies in the verses.

_____

_____

_____

Write three words to show how the righteous will be.

_____

_____

_____

My Praises

_____

_____

_____

_____

Pray About the Word

I am glad to be Your child, God. I pray that You help me to always follow in Your ways. I will hold onto Your Word all my life and never be Your enemy. Amen.

Use the Word

Pray each day this week for someone you know who needs God.

Song of Thanksgiving

Read the Word

Sing to the Lord with thanksgiving; make music to our God on the harp. He covers the sky with clouds; he supplies the earth with rain and makes grass grow on the hills. He provides food for the cattle and for the young ravens when they call.

— Psalm 147:7-9

Think About the Word

When did you last have a need that God didn't meet? He meets all of your needs. Maybe not all of your wants, but all of your needs. The verses above are a reminder that God provides for all of His creation. He made the sky and the clouds. He made the rain and causes it to make grass grow. This in turn provides for all the creatures that God created.

Live the Word

Write down at least ten needs that God has provided for you in the past week.

For example, you have at least one parent or caregiver who takes good care of you each day.

_____

_____

_____

_____

My Praises

_____

_____

_____

Pray About the Word

You have always provided for me, God. You know what I need before I ask. I am so thankful to You. Amen.

Use the Word

Write a letter to your parents and thank them for all they do for you. Tell them you are praying for them. (If you live with someone other than your parents, write a letter to your caregiver.)

_____

_____

_____

_____

⭐

Praise You in Your House

Read the Word

These things I remember as I pour out my soul: how I used to go with the multitude, leading the procession to the house of God, with shouts of joy and thanksgiving among the festive throng.

— Psalm 42:4

Think About the Word

The verse above tells of when the psalmist was happy to go to the house of God. He is obviously having some problems that threaten to keep him from going to God's house.

Live the Word

Do you have times when you just don't feel like going to church? Perhaps you have a problem with a friend at church. Or maybe your family is having some trouble. Write how the psalmist went to God's house, beginning with the word "leading."

_____

_____

_____

_____

The psalmist is asking God to give him back that joy. God surely answered this prayer. He will also help you when you need to feel the kind of joy expressed in this psalm.

My Praises

_____

_____

_____

_____

Pray About the Word

God, I am a human being, with many faults. There are times when I don't feel the joy about going to Your house as written in this psalm. Help me to remember that all I need to do is ask and I will receive Your help. You will help me to shout with joy and thanksgiving. Amen.

Use the Word

Practice having an attitude of joy and thanksgiving each time you enter God's house. Remember to ask God for His help.

☆

Praise Out Loud

Read the Word

Come, let us sing for joy to the Lord; let us shout aloud to the Rock of our salvation. Let us come before him with thanksgiving and extol him with music and song. ("Extol" means "to praise highly.")

— Psalm 95:1-2

Think About the Word

It is not enough to be thankful in your heart and prayers. You must praise God out loud. That way, others will know how wonderful your God is.

Live the Word

Write at least two ways you can praise God out loud.

_____

_____

_____

My Praises

_____

_____

_____

_____

Pray About the Word

Father God, I will praise You any way that I can. I will shout, sing and tell others. I will come before You each day with thanksgiving. I love You, God, with all my heart. Amen.

Use the Word

Praise God in 3 different ways this week.

1. Write a prayer of thanksgiving.

2. Sing whenever you can. Use your favorite hymns or choruses.

3. Speak praises out loud. Praise God with your family or a friend.

chapter 2

Serve the Lord

Read the Word

Serve the Lord with fear and rejoice with trembling.

— Psalm 2:11

Think About the Word

God doesn't want you to be afraid of Him. He wants you to know about His power. He will strike down His enemies, which are those who do not follow Him or believe in Him. When you become God's child, you should serve Him and rejoice in Him. You don't have to be afraid of Him.

Live the Word

List three ways you can serve God.

_____

_____

_____

_____

_____

My Praises

_____

_____

_____

Pray About the Word

I love You, Lord. I want to serve You in anyway that I can. Show me a way to serve You each day. I will be waiting gladly to do as You want. Amen.

Use the Word

Which of the things you listed at left can you begin
to do this week?

_____

_____

Read John 3:16. How does this verse make you want
to serve God?

_____

_____

_____

_____

A Servant Redeemed

Read the Word

The Lord redeems his servants; no one will be condemned who takes refuge in him.

— Psalm 34:22

Think About the Word

Redeemed means "saved." Condemned means to "make judgment against." Refuge is "a safe place." This verse says that you are saved if you are God's servant. You are His special one, and you can find a hiding place in Him from the problems of the world. What a wonderful promise!

Live the Word

Who do you think God's servants are?

_____

_____

_____

My Praises

_____

_____

_____

Pray About the Word

God, I am so glad that I can find a safe place in You. I will be Your servant all my life. I want to serve You and please You. I want to tell others, so they may be saved also. Amen.

Use the Word

Write a praise prayer that tells God you are glad to be His redeemed servant.

_____

_____

_____

_____

Guide My Hand, Lord

Read the Word

May the favor of the Lord our God rest upon us; establish the work of our hands for us — yes, establish the work of our hands.

— Psalm 90:17

Think About the Word

All you do for God should be guided by Him. Established means "to be put into place." This verse asks God to help the work you do for Him be to guided by Him.

Live the Word

How can you allow God to guide all you do for Him?

_____

_____

_____

What might happen if you were to do things for God with an attitude that you don't need His guidance?

_____

_____

_____

My Praises

_____

_____

_____

Pray About the Word

Father, I really want all I do to be guided by You. That way You will be pleased with what I do, and You will be glorified. Amen.

Use the Word

Trace the outline of your hand on a piece of paper. Cut out the handprint. Write a promise to God that you will allow Him to guide all that you do for Him. Place the handprint where you can see it each day.

A Blameless Servant

Read the Word

(1) Blessed are they whose ways are blameless, who walk according to the law of the Lord. (2) Blessed are they who keep his statutes and seek him with all their heart. (3) They do nothing wrong; they walk in his ways. (4) You have laid down precepts that are to be fully obeyed. (5) Oh, that my ways were steadfast in obeying your decrees! (6) Then I would not be put to shame when I consider all your commands. (7) I will praise you with an upright heart as I learn your righteous laws. (8) I will obey your decrees; do not utterly forsake me. (11) I have hidden your word in my heart that I might not sin against you.

— Psalm 119:1-8, 11

Think About the Word

Read verses 1-8. These verses are saying that you need to obey God as closely as you can. List ways these verses say you can be blameless.

_____

_____

_____

_____

_____

_____

Live the Word

How can you do all of that? Read verse 11. There is your answer, right in God's Word. If you search God's Word and remember it, you can be a blameless servant.

My Praises

_____

_____

_____

_____

Pray About the Word

Father, Your Word tells me exactly how to be blameless in Your sight. You want me to obey Your laws and walk in Your ways. I will hide Your Word in my heart, God. Amen.

Use the Word

Memorize verse 11.

I Love Your Laws, God

Read the Word

Seven times a day I praise you for your righteous laws. Great peace have they who love your law, and nothing can make them stumble.
— Psalm 119:164-165

Think About the Word

The psalmist says he praised God seven times a day for His laws. You should love all of God's laws. They keep you from sinning and falling away from God.

Live the Word

Write below at least three important things you think God wants you to learn and obey. An example is: God wants me to always tell the truth.

_____

_____

_____

_____

_____

My Praises

_____

_____

_____

_____

Pray About the Word

I will remember Your commandments, God. I will do my best to love and obey Your laws. Amen.

Use the Word

Read the Ten Commandments given in Exodus, chapter 20. Then read and memorize Psalm 119:168.

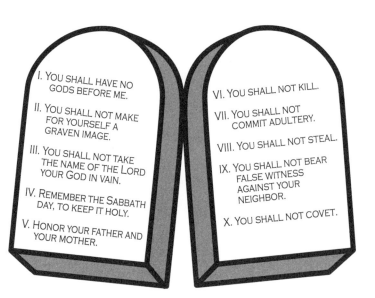

I. YOU SHALL HAVE NO GODS BEFORE ME.

II. YOU SHALL NOT MAKE FOR YOURSELF A GRAVEN IMAGE.

III. YOU SHALL NOT TAKE THE NAME OF THE LORD YOUR GOD IN VAIN.

IV. REMEMBER THE SABBATH DAY, TO KEEP IT HOLY.

V. HONOR YOUR FATHER AND YOUR MOTHER.

VI. YOU SHALL NOT KILL.

VII. YOU SHALL NOT COMMIT ADULTERY.

VIII. YOU SHALL NOT STEAL.

IX. YOU SHALL NOT BEAR FALSE WITNESS AGAINST YOUR NEIGHBOR.

X. YOU SHALL NOT COVET.

Clean Hands

Read the Word

The Lord has dealt with me according to my righteousness; according to the cleanness of my hands he has rewarded me. For I have kept the ways of the Lord; I have not done evil by turning from my God. All his laws are before me; I have not turned away from his decrees. I have been blameless before him and have kept myself from sin. The Lord has rewarded me according to my righteousness, according to the cleanness of my hands in his sight.

— Psalm 18:20-24

Think about the Word

What do you think "cleanness of my hands" means?

_____

_____

_____

(Read verse 23 again to find out, and write your answer on the lines below.

_____

_____

_____

What are some of the things the psalmist has NOT done?

_____

_____

_____

Live the Word

How can you use these verses to help you have "clean hands"?

_____

☆ _____

My Praises

_____

_____

_____

Pray About the Word

Lord, I want to be just like the psalmist. I will try to keep
Your ways. I will try to be blameless and keep myself from sin.
Thank You for rewarding Your righteous ones. Amen.

Use the Word

The Scripture at left is a long passage of verses. In order to
understand them and learn from them, read them again.

The Godly Pray

Read the Word

(5) Then I acknowledged my sin to you and did not cover up my iniquity. I said, "I will confess my transgressions to the Lord"—and you forgave the guilt of my sin. (6) Therefore let everyone who is godly pray to you while you may be found; surely when the mighty waters rise, they will not reach him. (7) You are my hiding place; you will protect me from trouble and surround me with songs of deliverance.

— Psalm 32:5-7

Think About the Word

Not only does God protect those who pray, He does something else important. Read verse 5 again. What does God do when you confess your sins?

_____

_____

_____

_____

Live the Word

In verse 5, there are three words that mean the same thing. Two of the words are "transgressions" and "iniquity." Can you guess the short word that means the same as these two longer ones?

_____

_____

_____

_____

My Praises

_____

_____

_____

Pray About the Word

God, I sometimes sin. It makes me feel so bad when I sin against You. I am so thankful that You are willing to forgive me when I confess my sins to You. You are my wonderful Father, my hiding place and my protector. I love you! Amen.

Use the Word

Write a poem about how good you feel when you know that God has forgiven you for something.

_____

_____

_____

_____

_____

_____

_____

He Hears My Prayers

Read the Word

Evening, morning and noon I cry out in distress, and he hears my voice.
— Psalm 55:17

Think About the Word

God hears your prayers no matter what time of day you pray. It is a comfort to know that He always hears.

Live the Word

List some ways you can serve God by praying to Him.

_____

_____

_____

_____

_____

My Praises

_____

_____

_____

_____

_____

Pray About the Word

Heavenly Father, I love to talk to You. I know You always hear my voice and will answer me. I love You. Amen.

Use the Word

Write a television commercial to convince people that God hears and answers prayer.

_____

_____

_____

Your Flawless Word

Read the Word

As for God, his way is perfect; the word of the Lord is flawless.

— Psalm 18:30

Think About the Word

God's Word is flawless. That means "without mistakes, without fault." Perfect, just like God Himself.

Live the Word

How many times a week do you read God's Word?

_____

What is your favorite Bible story?

_____

_____

_____

What is your favorite Bible verse?

_____

_____

_____

My Praises

_____

_____

_____

_____

Pray About the Word

Father, there is absolutely nothing else in this world that I can count on being perfect and flawless. Your Word is flawless. You are perfect. I love to read Your Word and learn more about You. Amen.

Use the Word

Read Psalms 18:30-32 Write down some ways you can use God's Word to stand strong in today's world.

A Light for My Path

Read the Word

(105) Your word is a lamp to my feet and a light for my path.
(169) Give me understanding according to your word.

— Psalm 119:105, 169

Think About the Word

God's Word is a lamp for your feet and a light for your path.
This means that you can be guided through your whole life
with God's Word. Even when the way seems dark and unsure,
God's Word will light the way for you.

Live the Word

Did you ever try to put together a toy or something else that
came unassembled from the store? You expected the wonderful
toy that you saw on the shelf. However, when you opened the
box at home, you saw a big pile of parts, screws, bolts and
plastic pieces. But, of course, you also received an instruction
book. Without this little guide, you would be clueless as how to
put together your wonderful toy. In verse 169, the psalmist is
asking God to help Him understand the Word. You should also
ask for help in understanding the Word.

My Praises

_____

_____

_____

_____

Pray About the Word

God, I am very thankful for Your instruction book about life. I love Your Word. I promise to read the Bible. Amen.

Use the Word

Memorize both of today's verses to help you remember how important it is to read and study God's Word.

Worship with Gladness

Read the Word

(1) Shout for joy to the Lord, all the earth. (2) Worship the Lord with gladness; come before him with joyful songs. (3) Know that the Lord is God. It is he who made us, and we are his; we are his people, the sheep of his pasture. (4) Enter his gates with thanksgiving and his courts with praise; give thanks to him and praise his name. (5) For the Lord is good and his love endures forever; his faithfulness continues through all generations.

— Psalm 100

Think About the Word

What a wonderful passage of Scripture! God made you and you are His. That verse should erase any doubt that you are God's own child.

Live the Word

Write the first words of verses 1, 2, 3, 4.

_____

_____

_____

What wonderful praise words!

Write out verse 5.

_____

_____

_____

My Praises

_____

_____

_____

Pray About the Word

I shout for joy, Lord. I worship with gladness. I know You are God. I enter Your courts with praise. I give thanks. I love You, Lord, with all my heart! Amen.

Use the Word

Write all of Psalm 100 and put it where you can see it everyday. Memorize the verses. You will be glad to have this wonderful psalm in your heart to help you through any difficult times in your life.

Give Glory

Read the Word

(1) Ascribe to the Lord, O mighty ones, ascribe to the Lord glory and strength. (2) Ascribe to the Lord the glory due his name; worship the Lord in the splendor of his holiness.

— Psalm 29:1-2

Think About the Word

The word ascribe is used several times. It means "to assign or give." Give the Lord glory!

Live the Word

Write some ways below that you can give God the glory. (One way is given in verse 2: worship.)

_____

_____

My Praises

_____

_____

_____

_____

_____

Pray About the Word

Lord, I will give You glory all my life. Please help me to remember that everything I do should be to glorify You. Amen.

Use the Word

Write below what you think glory means. Then look it up in a dictionary.

_____

_____

_____

_____

Write several words to describe God's glory.

_____

_____

_____

_____

_____

Worship in God's House

Read the Word

I rejoiced with those who said to me, "Let us go to the house of the Lord."

— Psalm 122:1

Think About the Word

This psalm is from David. He loved to worship God in many ways. This verse says he loved to go to God's house.

Live the Word

What do you like best about your own church?

_____

_____

_____

Have you ever visited another church? What did you like or dislike, compared to your own church?

_____

_____

_____

My Praises

_____

_____

_____

_____

Pray About the Word

God, I love to go to Your house and worship You. I love the songs and prayers. I love the lessons I learn. Thank You for providing Your house for us to worship in. Amen.

Use the Word

Look up Psalm 26:8. Write it here. This is a good verse to remember.

_____

_____

_____

_____

I Will Tell Others

Read the Word

One generation will commend your works to another; they will tell of your mighty acts. They will speak of the glorious splendor of your majesty, and I will meditate on your wonderful works. They will tell of the power of your awesome works, and I will proclaim your great deeds. They will celebrate your abundant goodness and joyfully sing of your righteousness.

— Psalm 145:4-7

Think About the Word

In these verses, not only will people tell others that they know about the greatness of God — they will tell generation after generation.

Live the Word

Your parents may take you to church. You may even have Bible studies and family prayer at home. Chances are, your parents learned about God and His ways from their parents. And their parents learned from their parents. So should the wonderful works of God be told from generation to generation. You will tell your children and they will tell their children — and on and on and on.

My Praises

_____

_____

_____

_____

Pray About the Word

God, I will tell those around me now about Your wonderful and great works. When I am an adult, I will tell my children and their children. I will continue to tell about You and praise You all my life. Amen.

Use the Word

Write down the names of every adult you can think of who has taught you about God, prayed with you or taken you to church. Then write down who you expect to tell these great things when you are an adult.

_____

_____

_____

_____

_____

_____

Tell of Your Righteousness

Read the Word

My mouth will tell of your righteousness, of your salvation all day long, though I know not its measure. I will come and proclaim your mighty acts, O Sovereign Lord; I will proclaim your righteousness, yours alone. My tongue will tell of your righteous acts all day long.
— Psalm 71:15-16, 24

Think About the Word

An easy way to remember what righteousness means is to make it a shorter word. Just think of "rightness."

Live the Word

The psalmist says his mouth and tongue will tell of God's righteousness. You should be that way, too. After all, God is so perfect and so right, how can you resist telling others about Him? Think of some bad ways to use your mouth and tongue. Write below how you can turn the bad ways into good by praising God.

_____

_____

_____

_____

My Praises

_____

_____

_____

_____

_____

Pray About the Word

Father, I am sometimes shy about telling others of Your love for me. Help me to be bolder and to share those things with others. Someone I know may need to hear about Your love today. Amen.

Use the Word

Read James 3:9-10. Write some comparisons between those verses and the ones from Psalms at left.

_____

_____

_____

_____

_____

Tell of Your Deeds

Read the Word

But as for me, it is good to be near God. I have made the Sovereign Lord my refuge; I will tell of all your deeds.

— Psalm 73:28

Think About the Word

Not only is the writer of this psalm ready to tell others about God; he says it is good to be NEAR God.

Live the Word

How can you stay near God and away from the things of the world? Write two or three ways below that you can think of.

_____

_____

_____

_____

My Praises

_____

_____

_____

_____

Pray About the Word

Father God, I love to be near You. I know You like to cradle me in Your love like a baby is cradled in her mother's arms. I will tell of all Your deeds. I will tell of all the blessings You have given me. Amen.

Use the Word

Make up a story about how a girl kept God close to her and was able to overcome some trouble. Example: Lisa's mom became very ill, and Lisa was able to help keep everyone praying for her mom.

chapter 3

I Trust You

Read the Word

(1) Vindicate me, O Lord, for I have led a blameless life; I have trusted in the Lord without wavering. (2) Test me, O Lord, and try me, examine my heart and my mind; (3) for your love is ever before me, and I walk continually in your truth.

— Psalm 26:1-3

Think About the Word

David is the psalmist who wrote these verses. Vindicate means "to take away the blame or prove worthy." David asks God to take away blame (the same as forgiving him). Just like David, you need to trust God without wavering, or without any doubt. Verse 2 asks God to test us, examine our hearts and mind.

Live the Word

Have you ever been around someone you didn't trust? Maybe you didn't know the person well. Or perhaps you have seen the person doing dishonest things. If you could examine others' hearts and minds, you would know whether to trust them. What are some ways you as a human can do that?

_____

_____

_____

_____

Write 3 things that the psalmist says he has done to prove he trusts God.

_____

_____

_____

My Praises

_____

_____

_____

_____

Pray About the Word

God, I trust You with my whole heart. Look into my heart and see how much I love and trust You. Amen.

Use the Word

Unscramble the words inside the heart to find good things. Would God find good things inside your heart today?

EECAP ☞ _ _ _ _ _

VELO ☞ _ _ _ _

HPOSIWR ☞ _ _ _ _ _ _ _

RSIAPE ☞ _ _ _ _ _ _

UTRHT ☞ _ _ _ _ _

HTAFI ☞ _ _ _ _ _

RTSUT ☞ _ _ _ _ _

OYJ ☞ _ _ _

☆

Trusting When I'm Afraid

Read the Word

(3) When I am afraid, I will trust in you. (4) In God, whose word I praise, in God I trust; I will not be afraid. What can mortal man do to me? (10) In God, whose word I praise, in the Lord, whose word I praise — (11) in God I trust; I will not be afraid. What can man do to me?
— Psalm 56:3-4 & 10-11

Think About the Word

The two sets of verses above are almost alike.

In whom should you trust?

_____

_____

_____

What do you praise?

_____

_____

_____

What do the verses say about people?

_____

_____

_____

Finish this line, "In God I _____; I will not be _____."

My Praises

_____

_____

_____

_____

Pray About the Word

God, there are times when I am afraid. I will remember these verses. I will not be afraid. I know You are taking care of me. I trust You, God. Amen.

Use the Word

Take out an American coin. Can you find some words on the coin that are also in these verses? Write those 3 words here.

_____

_____

_____

_____

Those Who Trust in Other Things

Read the Word

Some trust in chariots and some in horses, but we trust in the name of the Lord our God. I do not trust in my bow, my sword does not bring me victory; but you give us victory over our enemies, you put our adversaries to shame. In God we make our boast all day long, and we will praise your name forever. But man, despite his riches, does not endure; he is like the beasts that perish. This is the fate of those who trust in themselves, and of their followers, who approve of their sayings. Do not put your trust in princes, in mortal men, who cannot save.
— Psalms 20:7; 44:6-8; 49:12-13; 146:3

Think About the Word

Read all the verses above. Write some things others trust in, as listed in the verses.

_____

_____

Live the Word

Write some things people today trust in, rather than God.

_____

_____

_____

Write out the last part of Psalm 20:7.

But we trust in _____.

My Praises

_____

_____

_____

_____

Pray About the Word

God, I am as guilty as anyone of trusting in the wrong things. I sometimes would rather watch TV than help my mom or study the Bible. I know I should be learning, praising and serving. Help me to do better. Amen.

Use the Word

Write a fable about a girl who trusted in the wrong things. A fable is a made-up story that also teaches a lesson.

I Keep Trusting

Read the Word

Trust in the Lord and do good; dwell in the land and enjoy safe pasture. Delight yourself in the Lord and he will give you the desires of your heart. Commit your way to the Lord; trust in him and he will do this: He will make your righteousness shine like the dawn, the justice of your cause like the noonday sun. Be still before the Lord and wait patiently for him.

Psalm 37:3-7

Think About the Word

This portion of God's Word says to trust and keep doing good. Even when problems are all around you, you should continue to trust. You should continue to do good. To delight in the Lord means to surround yourself with His Word, with prayer and with praises to God.

Live the Word

How can you commit to the Lord?

_____

_____

_____

_____

What could God do to make your righteousness (rightness) shine out among all the bad around you?

_____

_____

_____

_____

My Praises

_____

_____

_____

_____

Pray About the Word

It is difficult to keep doing good sometimes, God. I see people sinning and hurting others all the time. I see people I once respected now getting into trouble. But I will trust You. I will obey Your Word and keep doing good. I will be patient. Amen.

Use the Word

The Scripture says if you delight yourself in the Lord, He will give you the desires of your heart. Write out one very strong desire that you have. Example: I want to be a Christian singer, God.

_____

_____

_____

_____

_____

_____

☆

My Strength

Read the Word

(1) I love you, O Lord, my strength. (2) The Lord is my rock, my fortress and my deliverer; my God is my rock, in whom I take refuge. He is my shield and the horn of my salvation, my stronghold.
— Psalm 18:1-2

Think About the Word

These verses summarize the whole theme for this chapter: Lord, You are everything to me.

Live the Word

Write some things that the verses say God is.

_____

_____

_____

_____

_____

My Praises

_____

_____

_____

_____

_____

Pray About the Word

I love You, Lord. You are everything to me. Amen.

Use the Word

Memorize verse 18:1. It is short and powerful! Write it here.

_____

_____

_____

_____

_____

☆

Praise to the Lord, My Strength

Read the Word

Praise be to the Lord, for he has heard my cry for mercy. (7) The Lord is my strength and my shield; my heart trusts in him, and I am helped. My heart leaps for joy and I will give thanks to him in song. (8) The Lord is the strength of his people, a fortress of salvation for his anointed one.

— Psalm 28:6-8

Think About the Word

God is to be praised and thanked for being your strength. When you trust Him, He will help you in whatever you do.

Live the Word

Write the two things the psalmist's heart does in verse 7.

_____

_____

_____

_____

My Praises

_____

_____

_____

_____

Pray About the Word

Father, I praise Your name. I sing with joy, for You are always there for me. I trust You. I love You very much. Amen.

Use the Word

Matthew 14:22-33 tells of someone who was able to do something unusual as long as he kept his eyes on the Lord. Read the story and draw a picture of it below.

You Hold My Hand

Read the Word

Yet I am always with you; you hold me by my right hand. You guide me with your counsel, and afterward you will take me into glory.
— Psalm 73:23-24

Think About the Word

Did you realize that God actually takes you by the hand and guides you? He has given you His Word to help guide your way. What more could you ask of your wonderful and caring God?

Live the Word

Write the four things that "you" (God) does for us in the verses above.

My Praises

_____

_____

_____

_____

_____

Pray About the Word

Thank You for being a God who cares enough to take me by the hand and guide me through my life. I want to please You, God. I love You. Amen.

Use the word

Read the verses at left again. List some situations where you might want God to be holding your hand.

_____

_____

_____

_____

My Hiding Place

Read the Word

(7) You are my hiding place; you will protect me from trouble and surround me with songs of deliverance. (8) I will instruct you and teach you in the way you should go; I will counsel you and watch over you.

— Psalm 32:7-8

Think About the Word

In verse 7, the psalmist is talking to God. In verse 8, God is speaking. God is your hiding place. He doesn't keep you from every bit of trouble that comes along. But, what He does promise is to help you through the troubles. He will guide you and help you make the right choices, if you let Him.

Live the Word

List at least three things that God will do for you, as written in verses 7 and 8.

_____

_____

_____

My Praises

_____

_____

_____

_____

Pray About the Word

God, I know You are my hiding place. When troubles come along, I will hide in You and let You help me work things out. I will listen while You teach me Your ways. Thank You for watching over me. Amen.

Use the Word

Write a prayer of your own to tell God You are glad He is your hiding place.

_____

_____

_____

_____

You Are Faithful

Read the Word

The Lord is faithful to all his promises and loving toward all he has made.
— Psalm 145:13

Think About the Word

Many times we make promises to someone, only to fail to keep
them. God never breaks a promise. He is faithful to keep every
one of them. He loves you very much.

Live the Word

Who is God loving toward?

_____

_____

_____

_____

My Praises

_____

_____

_____

Pray About the Word

God, You are truly everything to me. I am one of Your creations,
and You love me. You are faithful to keep every single promise
that You have made. Thank You. Amen.

Use the Word

What promises have you learned about by reading the Psalms?
List a few. Here is an example: God promises to be my strength.

_____

_____

_____

I Love You, Lord

Read the Word

I love the Lord, for he heard my voice.

— Psalm 116:1

Think About the Word

Don't you love to hear someone tell you, "I love you"? Those three words can wipe away hurt, fear, doubt and a lot of other bad things. God loves to hear those words, too. He deserves to be loved for all He does for you. But just because He is God is a good enough reason to say, "I love You, Lord."

Live the Word

Write two reasons you love the Lord.

_____

_____

_____

_____

My Praises

_____

_____

_____

_____

Pray About the Word

God, You are everything to me. I love You. I love You. I love You. Amen.

Use the Word

Find at least two other verses in Psalms that have the word LOVE. Write them here.

_____

_____

_____

_____

You Love Me with a Forever Love

Read the Word

(1) Give thanks to the Lord, for he is good; his love endures forever. (28) You are my God, and I will give you thanks; you are my God, and I will exalt you. (29) Give thanks to the Lord, for he is good; his love endures forever.

— Psalm 118:1, 28-29

Think About the Word

The first and last verses of Psalm 118 are exactly alike. God's love endures (lasts) forever! Can you think of anything else that will last forever?

Live the Word

Write the name of the oldest person you know.

_____

_____

Write the name of the oldest place you have ever seen.

_____

_____

Name an object that you know has been around for a long time.

_____

_____

Ask three people how long they think forever is.

_____

_____

My Praises

_____

_____

_____

Pray About the Word

Forever! God, You have promised to love me forever. I love
You, too. Amen.

Use the Word

Write a "diary" page about a forever friend. Do you have a
friend that promised to stick with you forever? Is she still your
friend now? Write what you feel a forever friend on earth is.

Unfailing Love

Read the Word

Let them give thanks to the Lord for his unfailing love and his wonderful deeds for men.

— Psalm 107:8

Think About the Word

What does unfailing love mean? It means that God's love will never, ever fail you. His way is perfect. His promises are true.

Live the Word

Read verses 15, 21 and 31 of chapter 107. What is interesting about them?

_____

_____

_____

_____

_____

My Praises

_____

_____

_____

_____

_____

Pray About the Word

Father in heaven, I love You very much. I can never begin to express to You just how much I love You. You are unfailing in Your love to me. Nobody here on earth could ever claim that kind of love for me. I am glad to be Your child. Amen.

Use the Word

Read verse 43 of chapter 107. Write it here.

_____

_____

_____

_____

Even Me

Read the Word

Give thanks to the Lord, for he is good. Give thanks to the God of heaven.

— Psalm 136: 1, 26

Think About the Word

Chapter 136 in Psalms is filled with reasons to give thanks to God. His love is so great, His power so mighty. Isn't it awesome to think that this great and wonderful God loves even you and me?

Love the Word

Read the whole chapter. Write the four words that follow each verse.

_____

_____

_____

_____

Write at least three great things this chapter tells about God.

_____

_____

_____

My Praises

_____

_____

_____

Pray About the Word

God, You have kept Your people in Your care for hundreds and hundreds of years. You love me just as if I were the only person You created. I love You, too.

Use the Word

Read the chapter again. Choose one of the Bible stories you recognize from the verses and write out the story. Example: Verse 5 says God made the heavens. You could write how God created the heavens, stars, sun and moon.

My Rock and My Salvation

Read the Word

(1) My soul finds rest in God alone; my salvation comes from him. (2) He alone is my rock and my salvation; he is my fortress, I will never be shaken. (6) He alone is my rock and my salvation; he is my fortress, I will not be shaken. (7) My salvation and my honor depend on God; he is my mighty rock, my refuge. (8) Trust in him at all times.

— Psalm 62: 1-2, 6-8

Think About the Word

Read all the verses. What do verses 2 and 6 have in common? A rock is something that is very sturdy, almost unmoveable. God, of course, is certainly an unmoveable rock. Salvation means that you are saved by God's power. In the Psalms, salvation can mean two things: One, you are saved in times of trouble, and two, you are God's own saved person and are chosen to be with Him in heaven at the end of time.

Live the Word

Which words or phrases in the Scripture tell you you are safe in God's care?

_____

_____

_____

_____

Write about how God is your rock.

_____

_____

_____

_____

My Praises

_____

_____

_____

_____

Pray About the Word

God, sometimes my world gets scary. I am glad to know I have an unmoveable rock to lean on. I can never thank You enough for being that rock. I am also very thankful to know I am saved. I love You. Amen.

Use the Word

Pretend that you have to write a sermon for your preacher. Tell the people of your church how God is your rock and salvation. Tell them how to have God as their own rock and salvation.

_____

_____

_____

_____

Rejoice in salvation

Read the Word

I trust in your unfailing love; my heart rejoices in your salvation.
— Psalm 13:5

Think About the Word

This short verse has a lot of power. God's unfailing love is trustworthy. You can depend on it. His salvation is also unfailing. You can be sure that you are saved. Your heart can be filled with joy all of your life, no matter what is happening around you. Why? Because you know without a doubt that you are God's saved. You have salvation in Him.

Live the Word

Write at least one reason you will be able to rejoice all your life.

_____

_____

_____

My Praises

_____

_____

_____

Pray About the Word

Saved! Lord, I am one of Your saved! That makes me feel like just shouting to the whole world. No matter what happens in my life, I am and will always be Your saved child! I promise to follow Your ways. Amen.

Use the Word

Write a newspaper article to tell the world that they, too, can have salvation.

_____

_____

_____

_____

_____

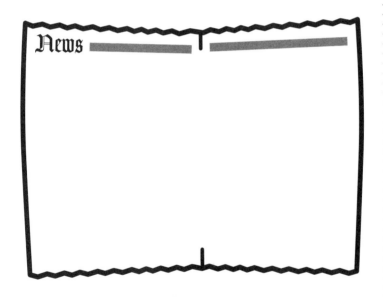

My Savior

Read the Word

(1) The earth is the Lord's, and everything in it, the world, and all who live in it; (2) for he founded it upon the seas and established it upon the waters. (3) Who may ascend the hill of the Lord? Who may stand in his holy place? (4) He who has clean hands and a pure heart, who does not lift up his soul to an idol or swear by what is false. (5) He will receive blessing from the Lord and vindication from God his Savior.

— Psalm 24:1-5

Think About the Word

This whole world is God's. He put everyone here. But everyone on earth will not go to heaven. Verse 3 asks two questions. Write them here.

_____

_____

_____

Write the answers here.

_____

_____

_____

Vindication means "to be proven blameless." You are cleared of your sins when you confess them to God and try to follow His ways. Who do you receive that vindication from? From God, your Savior!

Live the Word

Did you ever have a club in which you only allowed certain people? What rules did you have to decide who could belong?

_____

_____

What are the rules to be in God's "club"?

_____

_____

_____

My Praises

_____

_____

_____

Pray About the Word

Dear Savior and God, I am so thankful to be blameless in Your sight. I will try my best to follow Your ways. I am so glad You are my Savior. Amen.

Use the Word

Draw the outline of your hand on a piece of paper. Cut it out and make three more. Draw and cut out a heart. Write verses 1-5 on the hands and heart, one verse to each cutout. Hang with string on a clothes hanger to make a memory mobile.

☆

Saved by Your Son

Read the Word

Let your hand rest on the man at your right hand, the son of man you have raised up for yourself.

— Psalm 80:17

Think About the Word

This verse is telling something that actually happened after it was written. This is called prophecy — telling something that has not yet happened.

Live the Word

Write whom you think the verse is telling us about.

_____

_____

_____

_____

_____

My Praises

_____

_____

_____

_____

_____

Pray About the Word

God, I am thankful to be one of Your saved children. It is comforting to read this Psalm about the future coming of Your Son, Jesus. Thank You for providing a Savior for us.

Use the Word

Look up another place in the Old Testament that tells of the future coming of Jesus as our Lord and Savior — Isaiah 9:1-7. Write out Isaiah 9:6.

_____

_____

_____

_____

My Father

Read the Word

He will call out to me, "You are my Father, my God, the Rock my Savior."

— Psalm 89:26

Think About the Word

Write the four names listed in this verse that you might call God.

_____

_____

_____

_____

Live the Word

What does it mean to you to have a Father in heaven, so powerful, so loving and so interested in everything you do?

_____

_____

_____

_____

My Praises

_____

_____

_____

_____

_____

Pray About the Word

Lord, You are everything to me. You are my Father, my God, my Rock and my Savior. You are all that I need. Amen.

Use the Word

Make a "Father's Day" card for God on a separate piece of paper.

A Father to the Fatherless

Read the Word

His name is the Lord — and rejoice before him. A father to the fatherless, a defender of widows, is God in his holy dwelling. God sets the lonely in families, he leads forth the prisoners with singing.
— Psalm 68:4-6

Think About the Word

Do you know anyone who is fatherless? Maybe you don't have a father in your home. God wants to be that Father for you. If you know someone else who doesn't have a father in the home, tell him or her about God. Notice that the verse also says that God takes care of widows (a widow is a woman whose husband has died). He gives a family to the lonely. God even takes care of prisoners. God is truly everything to everyone.

Live the Word

In what ways is God your Father?

_____

How does God help lonely people?

_____

_____

_____

My Praises

_____

_____

_____

_____

Pray About the Word

Father, I love to call You that. Father, God. My Lord. My Savior. I love You. I will tell others about You so they, too, may fall in love with You. Amen.

Use the Word

Write an invitation to a fatherless child. Tell the child that God wants to be her Father. Then write an invitation to a lonely person. Tell the person that God wants to provide a family to take away the loneliness.

To: You
From: God

I am a Father to the fatherless. I know you and Love you.

My Protector

Read the Word

(1) The Lord is my light and my salvation — whom shall I fear? The Lord is the stronghold of my life — of whom shall I be afraid? (2) When evil men advance against me to devour my flesh, when my enemies and my foes attack me, they will stumble and fall. (3) Though an army besiege me, my heart will not fear; though war break out against me, even then will I be confident. (4) One thing I ask of the Lord, this is what I seek: that I may dwell in the house of the Lord all the days of my life, to gaze upon the beauty of the Lord and to seek him in his temple. (5) For in the day of trouble he will keep me safe in his dwelling; he will hide me in the shelter of his tabernacle and set me high upon a rock. (6) Then my head will be exalted above the enemies who surround me; at his tabernacle will I sacrifice with shouts of joy; I will sing and make music to the Lord.

— Psalm 27:1-6

Think About the Word

With God on your side, why should you have anything to be afraid of? God promises to keep you from the enemies around you. Just think how upset your enemies will be when they try to destroy your faith in God and you just shout and sing praises to God!

Live the Word

Write some things today that might be your enemies. (Not just people.)

_____

_____

_____

In verse 6, what will our heads be above?

_____

_____

My Praises

_____

_____

_____

Pray About the Word

You are my light and my salvation, God. I will not be afraid of
life's problems or the people who try to destroy my faith in
You. I will dwell in Your presence all my life. Amen.

Use the Word

Choose at least one of these verses to memorize. You may want
to write each of them down and place each where you can see it
everyday — Psalm 27:1, 4 or 6.

My Shepherd

Read the Word

(1) The Lord is my shepherd, I shall not be in want. (2) He makes me lie down in green pastures, he leads me beside quiet waters, (3) he restores my soul. He guides me in paths of righteousness for his name's sake. (4) Even though I walk through the valley of the shadow of death, I will fear no evil, for you are with me; your rod and your staff, they comfort me. (5) You prepare a table before me in the presence of my enemies. You anoint my head with oil; my cup overflows. (6) Surely goodness and love will follow me all the days of my life, and I will dwell in the house of the Lord forever.

— Psalm 23

Think About the Word

David wrote these psalms. He was expressing his love for God, as well as his thankfulness that God was always watching over him. In this chapter, David tells that God is everything to him. Just as God is everything to you.

Live the Word

Write three things that God has done in the verses David wrote.

_____

_____

_____

_____

Write three things that God does for you.

_____

_____

_____

_____

My Praises

_____

_____

_____

Pray About the Word

You do everything for me, Lord. You give me everything. You
are everything. I give praise to You! Amen.

Use the Word

Write verse 23:2 below. Draw a picture to illustrate the verse.

_____

_____

_____

Chapter 4

Praise Your Holy Name

Read the Word

Yet you are enthroned as the Holy One; you are the praise of Israel. In you our fathers put their trust; they trusted and you delivered them. They cried to you and were saved; in you they trusted and were not disappointed.

— Psalm 22:3-5

Think About the Word

The psalmist, David, says in this passage that he knows God is holy. God has proven Himself over and over. He has helped others in the generations before David's time. God has taken care of the people from David's time to today. And God will take care of His people even after your time on earth. People have trusted God down through the ages. He has never disappointed, and He never will.

Live the Word

How do people disappoint you?

_____

_____

_____

_____

For what do you need to be trusting God right now?

_____

_____

_____

My Praises

_____

_____

_____

Pray about the Word

God, I am glad to read that David and those before him in the Bible put their trust in You. When I know how You have cared for Your people throughout all of time, I know You will also take care of me. I praise Your holy name. Amen.

Use the Word

Read these verses about our holy God: Psalm 30:4 and 97:12.

My God Is Holy

Read the Word

*Let them praise your great and awesome name — he is holy. Exalt the
Lord our God and worship at his footstool; he is holy. Exalt the Lord our
God and worship at his holy mountain, for the Lord our God is holy.*
— Psalm 99:3, 5, 9

Think About the Word

The Lord our God is holy! Exalt means "to glorify or praise."
We are told in these verses to praise and worship God.

Live the Word

The entire chapter of Psalm 99 tells several reasons to know our
God is holy. Read the chapter and list some of the reasons here:

_____

_____

_____

_____

_____

My Praises

_____

_____

_____

_____

_____

Pray About the Word

I will praise You, holy God. I will tell others how holy and awesome You are. Amen.

Use the Word

Make a poster for your room. Use markers or crayons. Write on the poster THE LORD OUR GOD IS HOLY. With different colors, write words to describe holy God.

How Majestic Is Your Name!

Read the Word

O Lord, our Lord, how majestic is your name in all the earth!

— Psalm 8:9

Think About the Word

This is an easy verse to memorize. Say it over a few times.

Live the Word

What does the word majestic mean to you? Write some majestic descriptions here.

_____

_____

_____

What makes God majestic?

_____

_____

_____

My Praises

_____

_____

_____

Pray About the Word

Majestic! That is what Your name is, Lord. Nothing in all the universe can compare to Your majestic name! Amen.

Use the Word

Write a cinquain poem. A cinquain has 5 lines, and is written in this order:

Line one is 1 word that tells what the poem is about.
The words in the other lines tell something about the first word.
Line two has 2 words.
Line three has 3 words.
Line four has 4 words.
Line five has one or more words that has the same meaning as line one.

Here is an example:

God

Our Creator

Ruler of earth

Worthy of our Praise

Lord

_____

_____

_____

_____

_____

☆

The Majesty of My God

Read the Word

Praise the Lord. I will extol the Lord with all my heart in the council of the upright and in the assembly. Great are the works of the Lord; they are pondered by all who delight in them. Glorious and majestic are his deeds, and his righteousness endures forever. He has caused his wonders to be remembered; the Lord is gracious and compassionate. He provides food for those who fear him; he remembers his covenant forever. He has shown his people the power of his works, giving them the lands of other nations. The works of his hands are faithful and just; all his precepts are trustworthy. They are steadfast for ever and ever, done in faithfulness and uprightness. He provided redemption for his people; he ordained his covenant forever — holy and awesome is his name. The fear of the Lord is the beginning of wisdom; all who follow his precepts have good understanding. To him belongs eternal praise.

— Psalm 111

Think About the Word

Wow! What wonderful verses to describe the majesty of God.

Live the Word

Write some of God's deeds that are written in these verses.

_____

_____

_____

Write some words that praise God.

_____

_____

My Praises

_____

_____

_____

_____

Pray About the Word

To You, dear Lord, belongs eternal praise. You are majestic.
Your works are majestic. Forever is how long I will praise You.
Amen.

Use the Word

Draw a crown on a piece of paper. Cut out the crown. Color it
in bright colors. Write on the back of the crown some of the
praise words in the verses. Examples: Holy and awesome.

My God Reigns

Read the Word

(1) The Lord reigns, let the earth be glad; let the distant shores rejoice. (9) For you, O Lord, are the Most High over all the earth; you are exalted far above all gods.

— Psalm 97:1, 9

Think About the Word

Have you ever heard a young child say, "My dad is bigger than your dad?" Or "My brother can beat up your brother?" These verses are saying that God is bigger than anyone. All of earth should be glad that God reigns, except, of course, those who don't obey Him. The gods in verse 9 are false gods, such as idols and other things people worship in place of God.

Live the Word

Over what does God not reign?

_____

_____

What do you need God's help with today?

_____

_____

My Praises

_____

_____

_____

Pray About the Word

You are my God, and You reign over everything else in all the universe. You are my hero, God! Amen.

Use the Word

Read the story of the prophets of Baal who tried to get their god, Baal, to start a fire on the altar (1 Kings 18:20-40). Draw a cartoon picture of the story below.

My God Reigns Forever

Read the Word

The Lord reigns forever; he has established his throne for judgment. He will judge the world in righteousness; he will govern the peoples with justice. The Lord is a refuge for the oppressed, a stronghold in times of trouble. Those who know your name will trust in you, for you, Lord, have never forsaken those who seek you.

— Psalm 9:7-10

Think About the Word

The verses above tell that God reigns forever. He will judge the world. Remember that righteousness means the same as rightness. God will judge everyone. You need to try to always be right with God and follow His ways.

Live the Word

God never forsakes those who follow Him. In what ways can you be a better follower of God?

_____

_____

_____

_____

My Praises

_____

_____

_____

_____

Pray About the Word

I will remain faithful and right, God. I am glad You reign forever! Amen.

Use the Word

Look up Psalm 146:10. Write it out here.

_____

_____

_____

_____

My God Is Everlasting

Read the Word

Before the mountains were born or you brought forth the earth and the world, from everlasting to everlasting you are God.

— Psalm 90:2

Think About the Word

God has always been and always will be. That is how you can know that you will live in heaven forever. Nothing else in your life will give you security more than knowing God. He is "everlasting." Read Psalm 90:4 to find out how long a thousand years is to God. Draw a circle. Where does the circle begin? Where does it end? This is a good example of God's everlasting presence.

Live the Word

Why are you glad to know that God is everlasting?

_____

_____

_____

_____

My Praises

_____

_____

_____

_____

Pray About the Word

God, it is good to know that You are everlasting. There are so many things in this world that I am just not sure about. I am glad that I can be sure of Your presence — Your everlasting presence. Amen.

Use the Word

Read Genesis 1:1-2 and John 1:1-3 to see what it was like before God created the earth and all the universe.

My God's Love Is Everlasting

Read the Word

(17) From everlasting to everlasting the Lord's love is with those who fear him, and his righteousness with their children's children — (18) with those who keep his covenant and remember to obey his precepts.
— Psalm 103:17-18

Think About the Word

Just like God Himself, God's love never ends. It is "from everlasting to everlasting" for those who obey His laws. God will love you for all eternity. You can be sure of that!

Live the Word

How long is the Lord's love?

_____

_____

_____

_____

_____

For whom is this love?

_____

_____

_____

My Praises

_____

_____

_____

Pray About the Word

Nothing else around me is as sure and long-lasting as Your love, Father. Thank You. Amen.

Use the Word

Memorize verse 17.

Mighty God

Read the Word

All you have made will praise you, O Lord; your saints will extol you. They will tell of the glory of your kingdom and speak of your might, so that all men may know of your mighty acts and the glorious splendor of your kingdom.

— Psalm 145:10-12

Think About the Word

All God has made will praise Him. Isn't that interesting? Not just those who love God, but all He has made. Someday, those who were God's enemies will be forced to praise Him. For now, you can tell others about His might. His kingdom is glorious. What a wonderful day it will be to witness the entire earth praising God!

Live the Word

Write some words that describe God's might.

_____

_____

_____

_____

My Praises

_____

_____

_____

_____

Pray About the Word

All will praise You someday, God. I will praise You now, and all my life. Amen.

Use the Word

Draw a picture of God's kingdom below.

My Creator

Read the Word

For you created my inmost being.

— Psalm 139:13

Think About the Word

God was present when you were being formed. He created you. God didn't just create Adam and Eve. God creates everyone just the way He wants.

Live the Word

Why does God make everyone different?

_____

_____

_____

_____

My Praises

_____

_____

_____

_____

Pray About the Word

I praise You for being my creator, Father. I am glad You made me the way You wanted me to be. Amen.

Use the Word

Write ten reasons you are glad God made you the way you are.

_____

_____

_____

_____

_____

_____

_____

_____

_____

_____

My God Is Faithful

Read the Word

To the faithful you show yourself faithful, to the blameless you show yourself blameless, to the pure you show yourself pure.

— Psalm 18:25-26

Think About the Word

If you have a friend who is not always honest, or sometimes just doesn't treat you right, how do you feel? Do you want to remain her friend? These verses tell that God is faithful to those who are faithful to Him. He is blameless (perfect) to those who try to be perfect. He is pure to those who try to be pure.

Live the Word

Write some ways you can be faithful to God.

_____

_____

_____

Write some ways God is faithful to you.

_____

_____

_____

My Praises

_____

_____

_____

Pray About the Word

God, I promise to be faithful to You. I know You are faithful in Your love for me. I know You are always there for me. Thank You. Amen.

Use the Word

Read and memorize Psalm 33:4.

Psalms to Memorize

His delight is in the law of the Lord, and on his law he meditates day and night.
Psalm 1:2

O Lord, our Lord, how majestic is your name in all the earth! You have set your glory above the heavens.
Psalm 8:1

The Lord is my rock, my fortress and my deliverer.
Psalms 18:2

The heavens declare the glory of God; the skies proclaim the work of his hands.
Psalm 19:1

May the words of my mouth and the meditation of my heart be pleasing in your sight, O Lord, my Rock and my Redeemer.
Psalm 19:14

The Lord is my shepherd, I shall not be in want.
Psalms 23:1

The Lord is my light and my salvation — whom shall I fear? The Lord is the stronghold of my life — of whom shall I be afraid?
Psalm 27:1

Many are the woes of the wicked, but the Lord's unfailing love surrounds the man who trusts in him.
Psalm 32:10

Blessed is the nation whose God is the Lord, the people he chose for his inheritance.
Psalm 33:12

Turn from evil and do good; seek peace and pursue it.
Psalm 34:14

The law of his God is in his heart; his feet do not slip.
Psalm 37:31

As the deer pants for streams of water, so my soul pants for you, O God.
Psalm 42:1

God is our refuge and strength, an ever-present help in trouble.
Psalm 46:1

Create in me a pure heart, O God, and renew a steadfast spirit within me.
Psalm 51:10

But you, O Lord, are a compassionate and gracious God, slow to anger, abounding in love and faithfulness.
Psalm 86:15

Shout for joy to the Lord, all the earth. Worship the Lord with gladness; come before him with joyful songs.
Psalms 100:1-2

Praise the Lord, O my soul; all my inmost being, praise his holy name.
Psalm 103:1

Praise the Lord, all you nations; extol him, all you peoples. For great is his love toward us, and the faithfulness of the Lord endures forever. Praise the Lord.
Psalm 117

I have hidden your word in my heart that I might not sin against you.
Psalm 119:11

Your word is a lamp to my feet and a light for my path.
Psalm 119:105

The Lord will keep you from all harm— he will watch over your life; the Lord will watch over your coming and going both now and forevermore.
Psalms 121:7-8

Give thanks to the Lord, for he is good. His love endures forever.
Psalm 136:1

Great is the Lord and most worthy of praise; his greatness no one can fathom.
Psalm 145:3

Let everything that has breath praise the Lord. Praise the Lord.
Psalm 150:6

In conclusion

Which Psalm did I enjoy most?

_____

How do I feel about God?

_____

_____

_____

_____

How do I know I am important to God?

_____

_____

_____

_____

What would I like to say to God?

_____

_____

_____

_____

What questions would I like to ask God?

_____

_____

_____

_____